Sara Teasdale, Love In Autumn & Other Poems

Poetry is a fascinating use of language. With almost a million words at its command it is not surprising that these Isles have produced some of the most beautiful, moving and descriptive verse through the centuries. In this series we look at individual poets who have shaped and influenced their craft and cement their place in our heritage. In this volume we look at the works of Sara Teasdale.

Sara Trevor Teasdale was born on August 8, 1884 in St Louis, Missouri. A woman of poor health it was only at 14 that she was well enough to begin school. Her education finished in 1903 at Hosmer Hall and her first poetry publication was in 1907 with her second book in 1911.

She was courted by various men among them Vachel Lindsay, a great poet but one who thought he could not provide a suitable standard of living for Sara so she married Ernst Filsinger in 1914. Sara's third poetry collection, Rivers to the Sea, was published in 1915 and was a best seller, being reprinted many times. A year later, in 1916 the married couple moved to New York City.

In 1917 she released the poetry collection Love Songs and the following year it won three awards: the Columbia University Poetry Society prize, the 1918 Pulitzer Prize for poetry and the annual prize of the Poetry Society of America.

By 1929 Sara was deeply unhappy and lonely so she moved interstate for three months, in order to gain a divorce. She did not wish to inform Filsinger, and only at the insistence of her lawyers as the divorce was going through did she - Filsinger was shocked and surprised.

After her divorce Sara remained in New York City and resumed her friendship with Vachel Lindsay, who was by this time married with children.

1931 Vachel Lindsay committed suicide. Two year later Sara to was dead - overdosing on sleeping pills. She is buried in the Bellefontaine Cemetery in St. Louis.

Many samples of our audiobooks are at our youtube channel http://www.youtube.com/user/PortablePoetry?feature=mhee   Complete volumes on many poets, themes and our other products can be purchased from iTunes, Amazon and other digital stores

Blue Squills
The Broken Field
But Not To Me
By The Sea
Central Park At Dusk
Chance
City Vignettes
Coney Island
Day And Night
Evening
The Faery Forest
A Fantasy
The Faults
Full Moon
Galahad In The Castle Of The Maidens
The Giver
Gramercy Park
Gray Eyes
Gray Fog
Guenevere
Helen Of Troy
Hidden Love
I Would Live In Your Love
In A Burying Ground
In A Cuban Garden
In The Metropolitan Museum
The India Wharf
Jewels
Less Than The Cloud To The Wind
Lessons
Lost Things
Love In Autumn
Lovely Chance
Madeira From The Sea
Mastery
A May Wind
The Net
Night In Arizona
Night Song At Amalfi
The Nights Remember
November
Other Men
Over The Roofs
Paris In Spring
Pierrot
The Prayer
Primavera Mia

Anadyomene

The wide, bright temple of the world I found,
And entered from the dizzy infinite
That I might kneel and worship thee in it;
Leaving the singing stars their ceaseless round
Of silver music sound on orbed sound,
For measured spaces where the shrines are lit,
And men with wisdom or with little wit
Implore the gods that mercy may abound.
Ah, Aphrodite, was it not from thee
My summons came across the endless spaces?
Mother of Love, turn not thy face from me
Now that I seek for thee in human faces;
Answer my prayer or set my spirit free
Again to drift along the starry places.

The Answer

When I go back to earth
And all my joyous body
Puts off the red and white
That once had been so proud,
If men should pass above
With false and feeble pity,
My dust will find a voice
To answer them aloud:

"Be still, I am content,
Take back your poor compassion,
Joy was a flame in me
Too steady to destroy;
Lithe as a bending reed
Loving the storm that sways her
I found more joy in sorrow
Than you could find in joy."

A Ballad Of Two Knights
Two knights rode forth at early dawn
A-seeking maids to wed,
Said one, "My lady must be fair,
With gold hair on her head."
Then spake the other knight-at-arms:
"I care not for her face,
But she I love must be a dove
For purity and grace."
And each knight blew upon his horn
And went his separate way,
And each knight found a lady-love
Before the fall of day.
But she was brown who should have had
The shining yellow hair
I ween the knights forgot their words
Or else they ceased to care.
For he who wanted purity
Brought home a wanton wild,
And when each saw the other knight
I ween that each knight smiled.

Beatrice
Send out the singers - let the room be still;
They have not eased my pain nor brought me sleep.
Close out the sun, for I would have it dark
That I may feel how black the grave will be.
The sun is setting, for the light is red,
And you are outlined in a golden fire,
Like Ursula upon an altar-screen.
Come, leave the light and sit beside my bed,
For I have had enough of saints and prayers.
Strange broken thoughts are beating in my brain,
They come and vanish and again they come.
It is the fever driving out my soul,
And Death stands waiting by the arras there.

Ornella, I will speak, for soon my lips
Shall keep a silence till the end of time.
You have a mouth for loving - listen then:
Keep tryst with Love before Death comes to tryst;
For I, who die, could wish that I had lived
A little closer to the world of men,
Not watching always thro' the blazoned panes
That show the world in chilly greens and blues
And grudge the sunshine that would enter in.
I was no part of all the troubled crowd
That moved beneath the palace windows here,
And yet sometimes a knight in shining steel
Would pass and catch the gleaming of my hair,
And wave a mailed hand and smile at me,
Whereat I made no sign and turned away,
Affrighted and yet glad and full of dreams.
Ah, dreams and dreams that asked no answering!
I should have wrought to make my dreams come true,
But all my life was like an autumn day,
Full of gray quiet and a hazy peace.
What was I saying? All is gone again.
It seemed but now I was the little child
Who played within a garden long ago.
Beyond the walls the festal trumpets blared.
Perhaps they carried some Madonna by
With tossing ensigns in a sea of flowers,
A painted Virgin with a painted Child,
Who saw for once the sweetness of the sun
Before they shut her in an altar-niche
Where tapers smoke against the windy gloom.
I gathered roses redder than my gown
And played that I was Saint Elizabeth,
Whose wine had turned to roses in her hands.
And as I played, a child came thro' the gate,
A boy who looked at me without a word,
As tho' he saw stretch far behind my head
Long lines of radiant angels, row on row.
That day we spoke a little, timidly,
And after that I never heard the voice
That sang so many songs for love of me.
He was content to stand and watch me pass,
To seek for me at matins every day,
Where I could feel his eyes the while I prayed.
I think if he had stretched his hands to me,
Or moved his lips to say a single word,
I might have loved him - he had wondrous eyes.

Ornella, are you there? I cannot see
Is every one so lonely when he dies?
The room is filled with lights - with waving lights
Who are the men and women 'round the bed?
What have I said, Ornella? Have they heard?
There was no evil hidden in my life,
And yet, and yet, I would not have them know
Am I not floating in a mist of light?
O lift me up and I shall reach the sun!

Bells
At six o'clock of an autumn dusk
With the sky in the west a rusty red,
The bells of the mission down in the valley
Cry out that the day is dead.
The first star pricks as sharp as steel
Why am I suddenly so cold?
Three bells, each with a separate sound
Clang in the valley, wearily tolled.
Bells in Venice, bells at sea,
Bells in the valley heavy and slow
There is no place over the crowded world
Where I can forget that the days go.

The Blind
The birds are all a-building,
They say the world's a-flower,
And still I linger lonely
Within a barren bower.
I weave a web of fancies
Of tears and darkness spun.
How shall I sing of sunlight
Who never saw the sun?
I hear the pipes a-blowing,
But yet I may not dance,
I know that Love is passing,
I cannot catch his glance.
And if his voice should call me
And I with groping dim
Should reach his place of calling
And stretch my arms to him,
The wind would blow between my hands
For Joy that I shall miss,
The rain would fall upon my mouth
That his will never kiss.

Blue Squills

How many million Aprils came
Before I ever knew
How white a cherry bough could be,
A bed of squills, how blue!
And many a dancing April
When life is done with me,
Will lift the blue flame of the flower
And the white flame of the tree.
Oh burn me with your beauty, then,
Oh hurt me, tree and flower,
Lest in the end death try to take
Even this glistening hour.
O shaken flowers, O shimmering trees,
O sunlit white and blue,
Wound me, that I, through endless sleep,
May bear the scar of you.

The Broken Field

My soul is a dark ploughed field
In the cold rain;
My soul is a broken field
Ploughed by pain.
Where grass and bending flowers
Were growing,
The field lies broken now
For another sowing.
Great Sower when you tread
My field again,
Scatter the furrows there
With better grain.

But Not To Me

The April night is still and sweet
With flowers on every tree;
Peace comes to them on quiet feet,
But not to me.
My peace is hidden in his breast
Where I shall never be,
Love comes to-night to all the rest,
But not to me.

By The Sea
Beside an ebbing northern sea
While stars awaken one by one,
We walk together, I and he.
He woos me with an easy grace
That proves him only half sincere;
A light smile flickers on his face.
To him love-making is an art,
And as a flutist plays a flute,
So does he play upon his heart
A music varied to his whim.
He has no use for love of mine,
He would not have me answer him.
To hide my eyes within the night
I watch the changeful lighthouse gleam
Alternately with red and white.
My laughter smites upon my ears,
So one who cries and wakes from sleep
Knows not it is himself he hears.
What if my voice should let him know
The mocking words were all a sham,
And lips that laugh could tremble so?
What if I lost the power to lie,
And he should only hear his name
In one low, broken cry?

Central Park At Dust
Buildings above the leafless trees
Loom high as castles in a dream,
While one by one the lamps come out
To thread the twilight with a gleam.
There is no sign of leaf or bud,
A hush is over everything
Silent as women wait for love,
The world is waiting for the spring.

Chance
How many times we must have met
Here on the street as strangers do,
Children of chance we were, who passed
The door of heaven and never knew.

City Vignettes

I

Dawn

The greenish sky glows up in misty reds,
The purple shadows turn to brick and stone,
The dreams wear thin, men turn upon their beds,
And hear the milk-cart jangle by alone.

II

Dusk

The city's street, a roaring blackened stream
Walled in by granite, thro' whose thousand eyes
A thousand yellow lights begin to gleam,
And over all the pale untroubled skies.

III

Rain at Night

The street-lamps shine in a yellow line
Down the splashy, gleaming street,
And the rain is heard now loud now blurred
By the tread of homing feet.

Coney Island

Why did you bring me here?
The sand is white with snow,
Over the wooden domes
The winter sea-winds blow
There is no shelter near,
Come, let us go.
With foam of icy lace
The sea creeps up the sand,
The wind is like a hand
That strikes us in the face.
Doors that June set a-swing
Are bolted long ago;
We try them uselessly
Alas, there cannot be
For us a second spring;
Come, let us go.

Day And Night

In Warsaw in Poland
Half the world away,
The one I love best of all
Thought of me to-day;

I know, for I went
Winged as a bird,
In the wide flowing wind
His own voice I heard;
His arms were round me
In a ferny place,
I looked in the pool
And there was his face
But now it is night
And the cold stars say:
"Warsaw in Poland
Is half the world away."

Evening

There was an evening when the sky was clear,
Ineffably translucent in its blue;
The tide was falling, and the sea withdrew
In hushed and happy music from the sheer
Shadowy granite of the cliffs; and fear
Of what life may be, and what death can do,
Fell from us like steel armor, and we knew
The beauty of the Law that holds us here.
It was as though we saw the Secret Will,
It was as though we floated and were free;
In the south-west a planet shone serenely,
And the high moon, most reticent and queenly,
Seeing the earth had darkened and grown still,
Misted with light the meadows of the sea.

The Faery Forest

The faery forest glimmered
Beneath an ivory moon,
The silver grasses shimmered
Against a faery tune.
Beneath the silken silence
The crystal branches slept,
And dreaming thro' the dew-fall
The cold white blossoms wept.

A Fantasy

Her voice is like clear water
That drips upon a stone
In forests far and silent
Where Quiet plays alone.

Her thoughts are like the lotus
Abloom by sacred streams
Beneath the temple arches
Where Quiet sits and dreams.
Her kisses are the roses
That glow while dusk is deep
In Persian garden closes
Where Quiet falls asleep.

The Faults
They came to tell your faults to me,
They named them over one by one;
I laughed aloud when they were done,
I knew them all so well before,
Oh, they were blind, too blind to see
Your faults had made me love you more.

Full Moon
I listened, there was not a sound to hear
In the great rain of moonlight pouring down,
The eucalyptus trees were carved in silver,
And a light mist of silver lulled the town.
I saw far off the gray Pacific bearing
A broad white disk of flame,
And on the garden-walk a snail beside me
Tracing in crystal the slow way he came.

Galahad In The Castle Of The Maidens
(To the maiden with the hidden face in Abbey's painting)

The other maidens raised their eyes to him
Who stumbled in before them when the fight
Had left him victor, with a victor's right.
I think his eyes with quick hot tears grew dim;
He scarcely saw her swaying white and slim,
And trembling slightly, dreaming of his might,
Nor knew he touched her hand, as strangely light
As a wan wraith's beside a river's rim.
The other maidens raised their eyes to see
And only she has hid her face away,
And yet I ween she loved him more than they,
And very fairly fashioned was her face.
Yet for Love's shame and sweet humility,
She dared not meet him with their queenlike grace.

The Giver

You bound strong sandals on my feet,
You gave me bread and wine,
And sent me under sun and stars,
For all the world was mine.
Oh, take the sandals off my feet,
You know not what you do;
For all my world is in your arms,
My sun and stars are you.

Gramercy Park

The little park was filled with peace,
The walks were carpeted with snow,
But every iron gate was locked.
Lest if we entered, peace would go.
We circled it a dozen times,
The wind was blowing from the sea,
I only felt your restless eyes
Whose love was like a cloak for me.
Oh heavy gates that fate has locked
To bar the joy we may not win,
Peace would go out forevermore
If we should dare to enter in.

Gray Eyes

It was April when you came
The first time to me,
And my first look in your eyes
Was like my first look at the sea.
We have been together
Four Aprils now
Watching for the green
On the swaying willow bough;
Yet whenever I turn
To your gray eyes over me,
It is as though I looked
For the first time at the sea.

Gray Fog

A fog drifts in, the heavy laden
Cold white ghost of the sea

One by one the hills go out,
The road and the pepper-tree.
I watch the fog float in at the window
With the whole world gone blind,
Everything, even my longing, drowses,
Even the thoughts in my mind.
I put my head on my hands before me,
There is nothing left to be done or said,
There is nothing to hope for, I am tired,
And heavy as the dead.

Guenevere

I was a queen, and I have lost my crown;
A wife, and I have broken all my vows;
A lover, and I ruined him I loved:
There is no other havoc left to do.
A little month ago I was a queen,
And mothers held their babies up to see
When I came riding out of Camelot.
The women smiled, and all the world smiled too.
And now, what woman's eyes would smile on me?
I still am beautiful, and yet what child
Would think of me as some high, heaven-sent thing,
An angel, clad in gold and miniver?
The world would run from me, and yet am I
No different from the queen they used to love.
If water, flowing silver over stones,
Is forded, and beneath the horses' feet
Grows turbid suddenly, it clears again,
And men will drink it with no thought of harm.
Yet I am branded for a single fault.
I was the flower amid a toiling world,
Where people smiled to see one happy thing,
And they were proud and glad to raise me high;
They only asked that I should be right fair,
A little kind, and gowned wondrously,
And surely it were little praise to me
If I had pleased them well throughout my life.
I was a queen, the daughter of a king.
The crown was never heavy on my head,
It was my right, and was a part of me.
The women thought me proud, the men were kind,
And bowed right gallantly to kiss my hand,
And watched me as I passed them calmly by,
Along the halls I shall not tread again.
What if, to-night, I should revisit them?

The warders at the gates, the kitchen-maids,
The very beggars would stand off from me,
And I, their queen, would climb the stairs alone,
Pass through the banquet-hall, a loathed thing,
And seek my chambers for a hiding-place,
And I should find them but a sepulchre,
The very rushes rotted on the floors,
The fire in ashes on the freezing hearth.
I was a queen, and he who loved me best
Made me a woman for a night and day,
And now I go unqueened forevermore.
A queen should never dream on summer eves,
When hovering spells are heavy in the dusk:
I think no night was ever quite so still,
So smoothly lit with red along the west,
So deeply hushed with quiet through and through.
And strangely clear, and deeply dyed with light,
The trees stood straight against a paling sky,
With Venus burning lamp-like in the west.
I walked alone amid a thousand flowers,
That drooped their heads and drowsed beneath the dew,
And all my thoughts were quieted to sleep.
Behind me, on the walk, I heard a step
I did not know my heart could tell his tread,
I did not know I loved him till that hour.
Within my breast I felt a wild, sick pain,
The garden reeled a little, I was weak,
And quick he came behind me, caught my arms,
That ached beneath his touch; and then I swayed,
My head fell backward and I saw his face.
All this grows bitter that was once so sweet,
And many mouths must drain the dregs of it.
But none will pity me, nor pity him
Whom Love so lashed, and with such cruel thongs.

Helen Of Troy
Wild flight on flight against the fading dawn
The flames' red wings soar upward duskily.
This is the funeral pyre and Troy is dead
That sparkled so the day I saw it first,
And darkened slowly after. I am she
Who loves all beauty - yet I wither it.
Why have the high gods made me wreak their wrath
Forever since my maidenhood to sow
Sorrow and blood about me? Lo, they keep
Their bitter care above me even now.

It was the gods who led me to this lair,
That tho' the burning winds should make me weak,
They should not snatch the life from out my lips.
Olympus let the other women die;
They shall be quiet when the day is done
And have no care to-morrow. Yet for me
There is no rest. The gods are not so kind
To her made half immortal like themselves.
It is to you I owe the cruel gift,
Leda, my mother, and the Swan, my sire,
To you the beauty and to you the bale;
For never woman born of man and maid
Had wrought such havoc on the earth as I,
Or troubled heaven with a sea of flame
That climbed to touch the silent whirling stars
And blotted out their brightness ere the dawn.
Have I not made the world to weep enough?
Give death to me. Yet life is more than death;
How could I leave the sound of singing winds,
The strong sweet scent that breathes from off the sea,
Or shut my eyes forever to the spring?
I will not give the grave my hands to hold,
My shining hair to light oblivion.
Have those who wander through the ways of death,
The still wan fields Elysian, any love
To lift their breasts with longing, any lips
To thirst against the quiver of a kiss?
Lo, I shall live to conquer Greece again,
To make the people love, who hate me now.
My dreams are over, I have ceased to cry
Against the fate that made men love my mouth
And left their spirits all too deaf to hear
The little songs that echoed through my soul.
I have no anger now. The dreams are done;
Yet since the Greeks and Trojans would not see
Aught but my body's fairness, till the end,
In all the islands set in all the seas,
And all the lands that lie beneath the sun,
Till light turn darkness, and till time shall sleep,
Men's lives shall waste with longing after me,
For I shall be the sum of their desire,
The whole of beauty, never seen again.
And they shall stretch their arms and starting, wake
With "Helen!" on their lips, and in their eyes
The vision of me. Always I shall be
Limned on the darkness like a shaft of light
That glimmers and is gone. They shall behold

Each one his dream that fashions me anew;
With hair like lakes that glint beneath the stars
Dark as sweet midnight, or with hair aglow
Like burnished gold that still retains the fire.
Yea, I shall haunt until the dusk of time
The heavy eyelids filled with fleeting dreams.
I wait for one who comes with sword to slay
The king I wronged who searches for me now;
And yet he shall not slay me. I shall stand
With lifted head and look within his eyes,
Baring my breast to him and to the sun.
He shall not have the power to stain with blood
That whiteness - for the thirsty sword shall fall
And he shall cry and catch me in his arms,
Bearing me back to Sparta on his breast.
Lo, I shall live to conquer Greece again!

Hidden Love
I hid the love within my heart,
And lit the laughter in my eyes,
That when we meet he may not know
My love that never dies.
But sometimes when he dreams at night
Of fragrant forests green and dim,
It may be that my love crept out
And brought the dream to him.
And sometimes when his heart is sick
And suddenly grows well again,
It may be that my love was there
To free his life of pain.

I Would Live In Your Love
I would live in your love as the sea-grasses live in the sea,
Borne up by each wave as it passes, drawn down by each wave that recedes;
I would empty my soul of the dreams that have gathered in me,
I would beat with your heart as it beats, I would follow your soul
as it leads.

In A Burying Ground
This is the spot where I will lie
When life has had enough of me,
These are the grasses that will blow
Above me like a living sea.

These gay old lilies will not shrink
To draw their life from death of mine,
And I will give my body's fire
To make blue flowers on this vine.
"O Soul," I said, "have you no tears?
Was not the body dear to you?"
I heard my soul say carelessly,
"The myrtle flowers will grow more blue."

In A Cuban Garden
Hibiscus flowers are cups of fire,
(Love me, my lover, life will not stay)
The bright poinsettia shakes in the wind,
A scarlet leaf is blowing away.
A lizard lifts his head and listens
Kiss me before the noon goes by,
Here in the shade of the ceiba hide me
From the great black vulture circling the sky.

In The Metropolitan Museum
Within the tiny Pantheon
We stood together silently,
Leaving the restless crowd awhile
As ships find shelter from the sea.
The ancient centuries came back
To cover us a moment's space,
And thro' the dome the light was glad
Because it shone upon your face.
Ah, not from Rome but farther still,
Beyond sun-smitten Salamis,
The moment took us, till you stooped
To find the present with a kiss.

The India Wharf
Here in the velvet stillness
The wide sown fields fall to the faint horizon,
Sleeping in starlight. . . .

A year ago we walked in the jangling city
Together . . . . forgetful.
One by one we crossed the avenues,
Rivers of light, roaring in tumult,
And came to the narrow, knotted streets.
Thru the tense crowd

We went aloof, ecstatic, walking in wonder,
Unconscious of our motion.
Forever the foreign people with dark, deep-seeing eyes
Passed us and passed.
Lights and foreign words and foreign faces,
I forgot them all;
I only felt alive, defiant of all death and sorrow,
Sure and elated.
That was the gift you gave me. . . .
The streets grew still more tangled,
And led at last to water black and glossy,
Flecked here and there with lights, faint and far off.
There on a shabby building was a sign
"The India Wharf " . . . and we turned back.
I always felt we could have taken ship
And crossed the bright green seas
To dreaming cities set on sacred streams
And palaces
Of ivory and scarlet.

Jewels
If I should see your eyes again,
I know how far their look would go
Back to a morning in the park
With sapphire shadows on the snow.
Or back to oak trees in the spring
When you unloosed my hair and kissed
The head that lay against your knees
In the leaf shadow's amethyst.
And still another shining place
We would remember - how the dun
Wild mountain held us on its crest
One diamond morning white with sun.
But I will turn my eyes from you
As women turn to put away
The jewels they have worn at night
And cannot wear in sober day.

Less Than The Cloud To The Wind
Less than the cloud to the wind,
Less than the foam to the sea,
Less than the rose to the storm
Am I to thee.
More than the star to the night,
More than the rain to the lea,

More than heaven to earth
Art thou to me.

Lessons
Unless I learn to ask no help
From any other soul but mine,
To seek no strength in waving reeds
Nor shade beneath a straggling pine;
Unless I learn to look at Grief
Unshrinking from her tear-blind eyes,
And take from Pleasure fearlessly
Whatever gifts will make me wise
Unless I learn these things on earth,
Why was I ever given birth?

Lost Things
Oh, I could let the world go by,
Its loud new wonders and its wars,
But how will I give up the sky
When winter dusk is set with stars?
And I could let the cities go,
Their changing customs and their creeds,
But oh, the summer rains that blow
In silver on the jewel-weeds!

Love In Autumn
I sought among the drifting leaves,
The golden leaves that once were green,
To see if Love were hiding there
And peeping out between.
For thro' the silver showers of May
And thro' the summer's heavy heat,
In vain I sought his golden head
And light, fast-flying feet.
Perhaps when all the world is bare
And cruel winter holds the land,
The Love that finds no place to hide
Will run and catch my hand.
I shall not care to have him then,
I shall be bitter and a-cold
It grows too late for frolicking
When all the world is old.
Then little hiding Love, come forth,
Come forth before the autumn goes,

And let us seek thro' ruined paths
The garden's last red rose.

Lovely Chance

O lovely chance, what can I do
To give my gratefulness to you?
You rise between myself and me
With a wise persistency;
I would have broken body and soul,
But by your grace, still I am whole.
Many a thing you did to save me,
Many a holy gift you gave me,
Music and friends and happy love
More than my dearest dreaming of;
And now in this wide twilight hour
With earth and heaven a dark, blue flower,
In a humble mood I bless
Your wisdom and your waywardness.
You brought me even here, where I
Live on a hill against the sky
And look on mountains and the sea
And a thin white moon in the pepper tree.

Madeira From The Sea

Out of the delicate dream of the distance an emerald emerges
Veiled in the violet folds of the air of the sea;
Softly the dream grows awakening - shimmering white of a city,
Splashes of crimson, the gay bougainvillea, the palms.
High in the infinite blue of its heaven a quiet cloud lingers,
Lost and forgotten of winds that have fallen asleep,
Fallen asleep to the tune of a Portuguese song in a garden.

Mastery

I would not have a god come in
To shield me suddenly from sin,
And set my house of life to rights;
Nor angels with bright burning wings
Ordering my earthly thoughts and things;
Rather my own frail guttering lights
Wind blown and nearly beaten out;
Rather the terror of the nights
And long, sick groping after doubt;
Rather be lost than let my soul
Slip vaguely from my own control

Of my own spirit let me be
In sole though feeble mastery.

A May Wind

I said, "I have shut my heart
As one shuts an open door,
That Love may starve therein
And trouble me no more."
But over the roofs there came
The wet new wind of May,
And a tune blew up from the curb
Where the street-pianos play.
My room was white with the sun
And Love cried out in me,
"I am strong, I will break your heart
Unless you set me free."

The Net

A diamond of a morning
Waked me an hour too soon;
Dawn had taken in the stars
And left the faint white moon.
O white moon, you are lonely,
It is the same with me,
But we have the world to roam over,
Only the lonely are free.

Night In Arizona

The moon is a charring ember
Dying into the dark;
Off in the crouching mountains
Coyotes bark.
The stars are heavy in heaven,
Too great for the sky to hold
What if they fell and shattered
The earth with gold?
No lights are over the mesa,
The wind is hard and wild,
I stand at the darkened window
And cry like a child.

Night Song At Amalfi

I asked the heaven of stars
What I should give my love
It answered me with silence,
Silence above.
I asked the darkened sea
Down where the fishers go
It answered me with silence,
Silence below.
Oh, I could give him weeping,
Or I could give him song
But how can I give silence,
My whole life long?

The Nights Remember

The days remember and the nights remember
The kingly hours that once you made so great,
Deep in my heart they lie, hidden in their splendor,
Buried like sovereigns in their robes of state.
Let them not wake again, better to lie there,
Wrapped in memories, jewelled and arrayed
Many a ghostly king has waked from death-sleep
And found his crown stolen and his throne decayed.

November

The world is tired, the year is old,
The little leaves are glad to die,
The wind goes shivering with cold
Among the rushes dry.
Our love is dying like the grass,
And we who kissed grow coldly kind,
Half glad to see our poor love pass
Like leaves along the wind.

Other Men

When I talk with other men
I always think of you
Your words are keener than their words,
And they are gentler, too.
When I look at other men,
I wish your face were there,
With its gray eyes and dark skin
And tossed black hair.
When I think of other men,
Dreaming alone by day,

The thought of you like a strong wind
Blows the dreams away.

Over The Roofs

I

Oh chimes set high on the sunny tower
Ring on, ring on unendingly,
Make all the hours a single hour,
For when the dusk begins to flower,
The man I love will come to me! . . .
But no, go slowly as you will,
I should not bid you hasten so,
For while I wait for love to come,
Some other girl is standing dumb,
Fearing her love will go.

II

Oh white steam over the roofs, blow high!
Oh chimes in the tower ring clear and free !
Oh sun awake in the covered sky,
For the man I love, loves me ! . . .
Oh drifting steam disperse and die,
Oh tower stand shrouded toward the south,
Fate heard afar my happy cry,
And laid her finger on my mouth.

III

The dusk was blue with blowing mist,
The lights were spangles in a veil,
And from the clamor far below
Floated faint music like a wail.
It voiced what I shall never speak,
My heart was breaking all night long,
But when the dawn was hard and gray,
My tears distilled into a song.

IV

I said, "I have shut my heart
As one shuts an open door,
That Love may starve therein
And trouble me no more."
But over the roofs there came
The wet new wind of May,
And a tune blew up from the curb
Where the street-pianos play.
My room was white with the sun
And Love cried out in me,
"I am strong, I will break your heart
Unless you set me free."

Paris In Spring

The city's all a-shining
Beneath a fickle sun,
A gay young wind's a-blowing,
The little shower is done.
But the rain-drops still are clinging
And falling one by one
Oh it's Paris, it's Paris,
And spring-time has begun.
I know the Bois is twinkling
In a sort of hazy sheen,
And down the Champs the gray old arch
Stands cold and still between.
But the walk is flecked with sunlight
Where the great acacias lean,
Oh it's Paris, it's Paris,
And the leaves are growing green.
The sun's gone in, the sparkle's dead,
There falls a dash of rain,
But who would care when such an air
Comes blowing up the Seine?
And still Ninette sits sewing
Beside her window-pane,
When it's Paris, it's Paris,
And spring-time's come again.

Pierrot

Pierrot stands in the garden
Beneath a waning moon,
And on his lute he fashions
A little silver tune.
Pierrot plays in the garden,
He thinks he plays for me,
But I am quite forgotten
Under the cherry tree.
Pierrot plays in the garden,
And all the roses know
That Pierrot loves his music,
But I love Pierrot.

The Prayer

My answered prayer came up to me,
And in the silence thus spake he:

"O you who prayed for me to come,
Your greeting is but cold and dumb."
My heart made answer: "You are fair,
But I have prayed too long to care.
Why came you not when all was new,
And I had died for joy of you."

Primavera Mia

As kings who see their little life-day pass,
Take off the heavy ermine and the crown,
So had the trees that autumn-time laid down
Their golden garments on the faded grass,
When I, who watched the seasons in the glass
Of mine own thoughts, saw all the autumn's brown
Leap into life and don a sunny gown
Of leafage such as happy April has.
Great spring came singing upward from the south;
For in my heart, far carried on the wind,
Your words like winged seeds took root and grew,
And all the world caught music from your mouth;
I saw the light as one who had been blind,
And knew my sun and song and spring were you.

The Princess In The Tower

I
The Princess sings:
I am the princess up in the tower
And I dream the whole day thro'
Of a knight who shall come with a silver spear
And a waving plume of blue.
I am the princess up in the tower,
And I dream my dreams by day,
But sometimes I wake, and my eyes are wet,
When the dusk is deep and gray.
For the peasant lovers go by beneath,
I hear them laugh and kiss,
And I forget my day-dream knight,
And long for a love like this.

II
The Minstrel sings:
I lie beside the princess' tower,
So close she cannot see my face,
And watch her dreaming all day long,
And bending with a lily's grace.

Her cheeks are paler than the moon
That sails along a sunny sky,
And yet her silent mouth is red
Where tender words and kisses lie.
I am a minstrel with a harp,
For love of her my songs are sweet,
And yet I dare not lift the voice
That lies so far beneath her feet.

III
The Knight sings:
O princess cease your dreams awhile
And look adown your tower's gray side
The princess gazes far away,
Nor hears nor heeds the words I cried.
Perchance my heart was overbold,
God made her dreams too pure to break,
She sees the angels in the air
Fly to and fro for Mary's sake.
Farewell, I mount and go my way,
But oh her hair the sun sifts thro'
The tilts and tourneys wait my spear,
I am the Knight of the Plume of Blue.

Red Maples
In the last year I have learned
How few men are worth my trust;
I have seen the friend I loved
Struck by death into the dust,
And fears I never knew before
Have knocked and knocked upon my door
"I shall hope little and ask for less,"
I said, "There is no happiness."
I have grown wise at last but how
Can I hide the gleam on the willow-bough,
Or keep the fragrance out of the rain
Now that April is here again?
When maples stand in a haze of fire
What can I say to the old desire,
What shall I do with the joy in me
That is born out of agony?

Refuge
From my spirit's gray defeat,
From my pulse's flagging beat,

From my hopes that turned to sand
Sifting through my close-clenched hand,
From my own fault's slavery,
If I can sing, I still am free.
For with my singing I can make
A refuge for my spirit's sake,
A house of shining words, to be
My fragile immortality.

Rispetto

Was that his step that sounded on the stair?
Was that his knock I heard upon the door?
I grow so tired I almost cease to care,
And yet I would that he might come once more.
It was the wind I heard, that mocks at me,
The bitter wind that is more cruel than he;
It was the wind that knocked upon the door,
But he will never knock nor enter more.

The River

I came from the sunny valleys
And sought for the open sea,
For I thought in its gray expanses
My peace would come to me.
I came at last to the ocean
And found it wild and black,
And I cried to the windless valleys,
"Be kind and take me back!"
But the thirsty tide ran inland,
And the salt waves drank of me,
And I who was fresh as the rainfall
Am bitter as the sea.

The Rose And The Bee

If I were a bee and you were a rose,
Would you let me in when the gray wind blows?
Would you hold your petals wide apart,
Would you let me in to find your heart,
If you were a rose?
"If I were a rose and you were a bee,
You should never go when you came to me,
I should hold my love on my heart at last,
I should close my leaves and keep you fast,
If you were a bee."

Roundel

If he could know my songs are all for him,
At silver dawn or in the evening glow,
Would he not smile and think it but a whim,
If he could know?
Or would his heart rejoice and overflow,
As happy brooks that break their icy rim
When April's horns along the hillsides blow?
I may not speak till Eros' torch is dim,
The god is bitter and will have it so;
And yet to-night our fate would seem less grim
If he could know.

The Shrine

There is no lord within my heart,
Left silent as an empty shrine
Where rose and myrtle intertwine,
Within a place apart.
No god is there of carven stone
To watch with still approving eyes
My thoughts like steady incense rise;
I dream and weep alone.
But if I keep my altar fair,
Some morning I shall lift my head
From roses deftly garlanded
To find the god is there.

Silence

We are anhungered after solitude,
Deep stillness pure of any speech or sound,
Soft quiet hovering over pools profound,
The silences that on the desert brood,
Above a windless hush of empty seas,
The broad unfurling banners of the dawn,
A faery forest where there sleeps a Faun;
Our souls are fain of solitudes like these.
O woman who divined our weariness,
And set the crown of silence on your art,
From what undreamed-of depth within your heart
Have you sent forth the hush that makes us free
To hear an instant, high above earth's stress,
The silent music of infinity?

The Silent Battle

He was a soldier in that fight
Where there is neither flag nor drum,
And without sound of musketry
The stealthy foemen come.
Year in, year out, by day and night
They forced him to a slow retreat,
And for his gallant fight alone
No fife was blown, and no drum beat.
In winter fog, in gathering mist
The gray grim battle had its end
And at the very last we knew
His enemy had turned his friend.

Snow Song

Fairy snow, fairy snow,
Blowing, blowing everywhere,
Would that I
Too, could fly
Lightly, lightly through the air.
Like a wee, crystal star
I should drift, I should blow
Near, more near,
To my dear
Where he comes through the snow.
I should fly to my love
Like a flake in the storm,
I should die,
I should die,
On his lips that are warm.

The Song Maker

I made a hundred little songs
That told the joy and pain of love,
And sang them blithely, tho' I knew
No whit thereof.
I was a weaver deaf and blind;
A miracle was wrought for me,
But I have lost my skill to weave
Since I can see.
For while I sang - ah swift and strange!
Love passed and touched me on the brow,
And I who made so many songs
Am silent now.

Spirit's House
From naked stones of agony
I will build a house for me;
As a mason all alone
I will raise it, stone by stone,
And every stone where I have bled
Will show a sign of dusky red.
I have not gone the way in vain,
For I have good of all my pain;
My spirit's quiet house will be
Built of naked stones I trod
On roads where I lost sight of God.

Spring In War Time
I feel the Spring far off, far off,
The faint far scent of bud and leaf
Oh how can Spring take heart to come
To a world in grief,
Deep grief?
The sun turns north, the days grow long,
Later the evening star grows bright
How can the daylight linger on
For men to fight,
Still fight?
The grass is waking in the ground,
Soon it will rise and blow in waves
How can it have the heart to sway
Over the graves,
New graves?
Under the boughs where lovers walked
The apple-blooms will shed their breath
But what of all the lovers now
Parted by death,
Gray Death?

Testament
I said, "I will take my life
And throw it away;
I who was fire and song
Will turn to clay."
"I will lie no more in the night
With shaken breath,

I will toss my heart in the air
To be caught by Death."
But out of the night I heard,
Like the inland sound of the sea,
The hushed and terrible sob
Of all humanity.
Then I said, "Oh who am I
To scorn God to his face?
I will bow my head and stay
And suffer with my race."

Those Who Love
Those who love the most
Do not talk of their love;
Francesca, Guenevere,
Dierdre, Iseult, Heloise
In the fragrant gardens of heaven
Are silent, or speak, if at all,
Of fragile, inconsequent things.
And a woman I used to know
Who loved one man from her youth,
Against the strength of the fates
Fighting in lonely pride,
Never spoke of this thing,
But hearing his name by chance,
A light would pass over her face.

Triolets
I
Love looked back as he took his flight,
And lo, his eyes were filled with tears.
Was it for love of lost delight
Love looked back as he took his flight?
Only I know while day grew night,
Turning still to the vanished years,
Love looked back as he took his flight,
And lo, his eyes were filled with tears.

II
(Written in a copy of "La Vita Nuova". For M. C. S.)
If you were Lady Beatrice
And I the Florentine,
I'd never waste my time like this
If you were Lady Beatrice
I'd woo and then demand a kiss,

Nor weep like Dante here, I ween,
If you were Lady Beatrice
And I the Florentine.

III
(Written in a copy of "The Poems of Sappho".)
Beyond the dim Hesperides,
The girl who sang them long ago
Could never dream that over seas,
Beyond the dim Hesperides,
The wind would blow such songs as these
I wonder now if she can know,
Beyond the dim Hesperides,
The girl who sang them long ago?

IV
Dead leaves upon the stream
And dead leaves on the air
All of my lost hopes seem
Dead leaves upon the stream;
I watch them in a dream,
Going I know not where,
Dead leaves upon the stream
And dead leaves on the air.

The Unchanging
Sun-swept beaches with a light wind blowing
From the immense blue circle of the sea,
And the soft thunder where long waves whiten
These were the same for Sappho as for me.
Two thousand years - much has gone by forever,
Change takes the gods and ships and speech of men
But here on the beaches that time passes over
The heart aches now as then.